Miscegenation

The Theory of the Blending of the Races, Applied to the American White Man and Negro

By David G. Croly

ISBN: 978-1-63923-755-5

Printed: February 2023

Published and Distributed By:
Lushena Books
607 Country Club Drive, Unit E
Bensenville, IL 60106
www.lushenabks.com

ISBN: 978-1-63923-755-5

TABLE OF CONTENTS.

INTRODUCTION.

The word is spoken at last. It is Miscegenation—the blending of the various races of men—the practical recognition of the brotherhood of all the children of the common father. While the sublime inspirations of Christianity have taught this doctrine, Christians so-called have ignored it in denying social equality to the colored man; while democracy is founded upon the idea that all men are equal, democrats have shrunk from the logic of their own creed, and refused to fraternize with the people of all nations; while science has demonstrated that the intermarriage of diverse races is indispensable to a progressive humanity, its votaries, in this country, at least, have never had the courage to apply that rule to the relations of the white and colored races. But Christianity, democracy, and science, are stronger than the timidity, prejudice, and pride of short-sighted men; and they teach that a people, to become great, must become composite. This involves what is vulgarly known as amalgamation, and those who dread that name, and the thought and fact it implies, are warned against reading these pages.

The author is aware that this book will call down upon itself a storm of contumely and abuse. He has withheld his name from the title page, not because he regrets any word in it, or is afraid to meet any argument against it ; but because he prefers that a great truth should spread by the force of its own momentum against the heart of the world. He is patient, he is confident. He appeals from the imperfect American of to-day, to the more perfect race that is yet to appear upon this continent. "If God," said the great German Astronomer, "could wait six thousand years before he revealed to me the laws which govern the heavenly bodies, I too can wait until men accept them as true."

NEW WORDS USED IN THIS BOOK.

Miscegenation—from the Latin *Miscere*, to mix, and *Genus*, race, is used to denote the abstract idea of the mixture of two or more races.
Miscegen—is used to denote an offspring of persons of different races, with the plural form, Miscegens.
Miscegenate—is used as the verbal form of the first mentioned word ; *e. g.* to *miscegenate*, *i. e.* to mingle persons of different races.
Miscegenetic—The adjective form.

But as the particular subject under discussion limits, in a certain view, the races that are to be intermingled, the following are suggested, to express the idea of the union of the white and black races :
Melaleukation—The abstract form.
Melaleukon (plural formed by adding *'s* to the word)—Substantive form.
Melaleuketic—Adjective form.

These words are derived from two Greek words, viz. : *Melas*, (μέλας), black ; and *Leukos* (λευκός), white. The word *Mignumi* (μίγνυμι), to mix, is understood, making the word Melamigleukation, which, aside from its difficulty of pronounciation, is ill adapted for popular use.

Reasons for coining these words—(1.) There is, as yet, no word in the language which expresses exactly the idea they embody. (2.) Amalgamation is a poor word, since it properly refers to the union of metals with quicksilver, and was, in fact, only borrowed for an emer gency, and should now be returned to its proper signification. (3.) The words used above are just the ones wanted, for they express the ideas with which we are dealing, and, what is quite as important, they express nothing else.

PHYSIOLOGICAL EQUALITY OF THE WHITE AND COLORED RACES.

The teachings of physiology as well as the inspirations of Christianity settle the question that all the tribes which inhabit the earth were originally derived from one type. Whether or not the story of Adam and Eve is accepted by all as absolutely true, the fact which it represents has been demonstrated by history, and by the latest discoveries bearing upon the origin of the human family.

The form of the skull varies in different parts of the earth, from the prognathous to the elliptical, while the color is of all shades between ebony and white. There are structural peculiarities, also, from the short, squat Esquimaux to the tall, lithe Patagonian. But despite skull, color, structure, the race is essentially one, and the differences depend wholly upon climate and circumstances. The reader would not thank us if we should burden this work with physiological arguments, but by examining the most popular books upon the subject it will be seen that the most profound investigation has proved, conclusively, not merely the unity of the race but the equality of the black with the white under the same advantages of education and condition.

There is no fact better established in the physical history of man than that color depends primarily upon temperature. The inhabitant of a northern clime is always white; of an extreme southern clime always black. The varieties of color exist between the two extremes. The Jews, who are tawny in their own country, are white in Northern Europe, with blue eyes and red beards; while in Borneo and Sumatra they are almost black. The Englishman or American who goes to the

East or West Indies soon has his liver affected, causing him in time to turn yellow. Indeed, Dr. Draper, of the New York University, attributes the change in the color of the skin entirely to the action of the liver. He ac. counts for the slight peculiarities of structure which distinguish the white from the black as being due to this important organ, and in his excellent work on Physiology explains the process minutely.

In reference to the general characteristics of races, he well says : "Submitted for a due time to a high temperature, any race, irrespective of its original color, will become dark, or if to a low temperature it will become fair. Under certain circumstances it will pass to the elliptical ; under others, to the prognathous form of skull. No race is in a state of absolute equilibrium, or able successfully to maintain its present physiognomy, if the circumstances under which it lives undergo a change. It holds itself ready with equal facility to descend to a baser or rise to a more elevated state, in correspondence with those circumstances. We confound temporary equilibration with final equilibrium."

Camper, one of the first authorities among anatomists and naturalists, than whom few men have received in their lives so many marks of distinction, delivered a lecture to the public, while occupying the Chair of Anatomy and Medicine in the University of Groningen, on the color of the skin of the negro. He first proposes to show that God created only one man, Adam, to whom all mankind owe their origin, whatever may be the traits of their countenance, or the color of their skin. He then examines the cause of diversity of color as to the exact situation of the peculiarity. "Examine the skin of this negro. You see that the true skin is perfectly white ; that over it is placed another membrane, called the reticnlar tissue, and that this is the membrane that is black ; and, finally, that it is covered by a third membrane, the scarf skin, which has been compared to a fine varnish lightly extended over the colored membrane, and designed to protect it. Examine also this piece of skin, belonging to a very fair person. You perceive over the true white skin a membrane of a slightly brownish tint, and over that again, but quite distinct from it, a transparent membrane. In other words, it clearly appears that the whites and the copper-colored have a colored membrane which is placed under the scarf skin and immediately above the true skin, just as it is in the negro. The infant negroes are born white or rather reddish, like those of other people, but in two or three days the color begins to change ; they speedily become copper-colored ; and by the seventh or eighth day, though never exposed to the sun, they appear quite black." He mentions that it is known that negroes in some rare instances are born quite white or are true Albinos ; sometimes, after being black for many years, they become piebald, or wholly white, without their general health suffering under the change. He also mentions another metamorphosis, which would not be agreeable to the prejudices of many amongst us ; it is that of the white becoming piebald with black as deep as ebony. He had seen only one case himself, but refers to other instances which had occurred under the observation of others. He agrees with Aristotle and Galen among the ancients, and with Buffon and others among the moderns, in thinking that temperature is the cause of color in the skin. With a long sojourn under a scorching sun, he says a white race would become black, and in opposite circumstances a black race become white. "Thus," he says, "I am satisfied with having proved by anatomical observation on our bodies, and particularly on our skin, that there is no room for believing that the race of negroes does not descend from Adam, as our own. Take all these things into consideration and you will find no difficulty in considering them genuine descendants of the common father of our race as you yourselves, nor will you hesitate with me to tender to the negro a brother's hand."

In the measurement of the skull the greatest importance is fixed by anatomists, in the comparison of races, upon the position of the great occipital foramen. Dr. Prichard says: "I have carefully examined the situation of the foramen magnum in many negro skulls, and in all of them it is found in precisely the place which Mr. Owen has pointed out as the general position of the occipital hole in the human skull. In those negro skulls which have the alveolar process very protuberant, the anterior half of the line above described is lengthened in a slight degree by the circumstance. If allowance is made for it, no difference is perceptible. * * * If a line is let fall from the summit of the head at right-angles with the plane of the basis, the occipital foramen will be found to be situated immediately behind it; and this is precisely the case in negro and European heads."

It has been remarked also that there is only the difference in the degree of crispation and coloring matter between the hair of the negro and the white. Prichard remarks that in the skull of the more improved and civilized nations among the woolly-haired blacks of Africa, there is comparatively slight deviation from the form which may be looked upon as the common type of the human head.

Baron Larrey says that the Arabian race furnishes the most perfect type of the human head, and yet the negro, so much maligned, is far superior to the Arab in every attribute of manhood.

Professor Draper says :

"It must be observed how forcibly the doctrine here urged of the passage of man from one complexion to another, and through successively different forms of skull in the course of ages, is illustrated by the singular circumstance to which attention has of late years been directed, of the gradual disappearance of the red-haired and blue-eyed men from Europe. Less than two thousand years ago the Roman authors bear their concurrent testimony to the fact, that the inhabitants of Britain, Gaul, and a large portion of Germany, were of this kind. But no one would accept such a description as correct in our own times. * * * The true reason is that the red-haired man has been slowly changing to get into correspondence with the conditions that have been introduced through the gradual spread of civilization—conditions of a purely physical kind, and with which the darker man was more in unison."

And upon the general subject of the unity of the race he comes to the following conclusions : "Wherever we look, man is the same. Stripped of exterior coverings, there is in every climate a common body and common mind. Are not all of us liable to the same diseases? Have not all a tendency to exist the same length of time? Is it the temperature of our body, the beat of our pulse, the respiration that we observe—are they not everywhere alike? Or, turning to the manifestations of the mind, is there not among all the tribes of our race a belief in the existence and goodness of God? in unseen agents intermediate between him and ourselves? and in a future life? Do we not all put a reliance in the efficacy of prayers, and all, in our youth, have a dread of ghosts? How many of us, in all parts of the world, attach a value to pilgrimages, sacrificial offerings, fastings, and unlucky days, and in our worldly proceedings are guided by codes of law and ideas of the nature of property! Have we not all the same fears, the same delights, the same aversions, and do we not resort to the use of fire, domestic animals, and wea pons? Do we not all expect that the differences which surround us here will be balanced hereafter, and that there are rewards and punishments? Is there not a common interpretation of all the varied forms of funeral ceremonies? a common sentiment of the sacredness of the tomb? Have we not always, and do we not everywhere set apart a sacerdotal order who may mediate for us? In our less advanced civilization, do we not all believe in sorceries, witches, and charms? It signifies nothing in what particular form our mental conceptions are embodied; it is the conception that concerns us, and not the aspect it has assumed. Thus equally do the views of the various nations demonstrate their innate belief in a future world—the undisturbed hunting-ground of the American Indian, the voluptuous Paradise and society of Houris of the Arabian, or the snow hut of the Esquimaux, in which the righteous feed on the blubber of whales."

II.

SUPERIORITY OF MIXED RACES.

If any fact is well established in history, it is that the miscegenetic or mixed races are much superior, mentally, physically, and morally, to those pure or unmixed. Wherever on the earth's surface we find a community which has intermarried for generations, we also find evidences of decay both in the physical and mental powers. On the other hand, wherever, through conquest, colonization, or commerce, different nationalities are blended, a superior human product invariably results.

The English people are great, because they are a composite race. The French, notwithstanding that they are called Celtic, are also originally of many diverse bloods. But its people have intermarried for so many years only among themselves, that it has gone very far in decay. The two most brilliant writers it can boast of are the melaleukon, Dumas, and his son, a quadroon. Take most of the eminent French names in literature, statesmanship, or war, and it will be found that they are mixtures of the modern French with the Germans or Italians. The great Napoleon was of an Italian family, and the present Napoleon is known to be the son of a Dutch admiral. Germany also is made up of a wide mixture of nations and races. The Slavic, Teutonic, and Saxon are all of diverse bloods, and the German of to-day is consequently of composite origin. The real superiority of the German over the Swede and Dane is due to the so-called purity of the Scandinavian race. The effect of a mixture of bloods is shown in a remarkable degree in the comparison between Northern and Southern Italy. The Sardinian is the controlling power to-day on the Italian peninsula, and why? Simply because all Northern Italy has been frequently overrun by the French and Austrian powers. The blood of the people has been fed from France, from Italy, from Switzerland, and from the Germanic races, which have successively occupied their country, either as conquerors, allies, mercenaries, or emigrants. The people of Sicily and Naples have had no such chance of interchange of blood ; and, as a consequence, they are probably the lowest people, except the Irish, in the scale of civilization in Europe. They are brutal, ignorant, and barbarous, lacking in everything which goes to make up a prosperous and enlightened community. The most promising nation in Europe is the Russian, and its future will be glorious, only because its people represents a greater variety of race than any other in Europe. The sources of power in its blood come not only from the Caucasian and European races, but also from the Asiatic. It would take pages to enumerate the tribes which are now known by the one generic name of Russian. That great empire includes every variety of race, with the exception of the extreme black. It is now the dominant, and is yet destined to be the master-power of Europe. The time is coming when the Russian dominion will stretch to the Atlantic ocean. Nor should such an event be dreaded. What the barbarians did for demoralized and degenerate Rome, the Russians will do for the effete and worn-out populations of Western Europe. These will be conquered. Their civilization, such as it is, will be overthrown ; but the new infusion of a young and composite blood will regenerate the life of Europe, will give it a new and better civilization, because the German, French, Italian, Spanish, and English will be mixed with a miscegenetic and progressive people.

The evil of a pure and the benefit of a mixed race is strikingly shown in the history of Spain. When the Moors overran the Spanish peninsula and gave their blood to the Spanish people, it resulted in a civilization as remarkable of its kind as anything which has existed in Europe. The traces of art, the monuments of great deeds done on the Spanish peninsula, are connected with the Moors, or rather with the blended Moors and Spaniards. To this day we hear of the glories of the Alhambra ; of the achievements in science, literature, and art, which resulted from the union between an Asiatic and a European people. The downfall of Spain dates from its cruel expulsion of the Moors from that peninsula. The pride of race, which led it to reject the rich blood of the Morisco, signaled the decadence of its power. Spain was once the greatest nation in Europe ; but the intermarriages between its people, and especially among the nobility and leading classes, rapidly deprived it of vital energy, and its history, until within the last few years, has been one of steady decline.

Whatever of power and vitality there is in the American race is derived, not from its Anglo-Saxon progenitors, but from all the different nationalities which go to make up this people. All that is needed to make us the finest race on earth is to engraft upon our stock the negro element which providence has placed by our side on this continent. Of all the rich treasures of blood vouchsafed to us, that of the negro is the most precious, because it is the most unlike any other that enters into the composition of our national life.

We will add a few casual instances and opinions from the testimony of travelers and students of physical history, in proof of the benefit of mixed bloods.

Dr. Prichard says : "Mixed breeds are very often superior, in almost all their physical qualities, to the present races, and particularly with so much vigor of propagation, that they often gain ground upon the older varieties, and gradually supersede them."

He mentions the fact that in some parts of Ireland, where the Celtic population are nearly unmixed, they are in general a people of short stature, small limbs and features; but where they are mixed with English settlers, or with the Lowlanders of Scotland, the people are remarkable for their fine figures, tall stature, and great physical energy.

Don Felix De Azara says that in Paraguay the mixed breed constitutes the great majority of the people termed Spaniards or White men, and they are a people superior in physical qualities to either of the races from which they have sprung, and much more prolific than the aborigines.

Pallas states that intermarriages of Russians and Tartars with the Mongolians are frequent, and that the children have agreeable and, sometimes, beautiful features, in great contrast to the purely Kalmuc or Mongol.

Moodie says that the offspring of Hottentot women and Dutch settlers are superior to the Hottentots, and many of them superior to the Dutch. The Griquas, or Griqua Hottentots, are a miscegenated race, descended from the Dutch colonists and aboriginal Hottentots, and are represented as a superior people.

Lawrence says: "The Persian blood is now highly refined by frequent intermixtures with the Georgians and Circassians, two nations which surpass all the world in personal beauty. There is hardly a man of rank in Persia who is not born of a Georgian or Circassian mother; and even the king himself is commonly sprung, on the female side, from one or other of these countries. As it is long since this mixture commenced, the Persian women have been very handsome and beautiful, though they do not rival the ladies of Georgia. The men are generally tall and erect; their complexion is ruddy and vigorous, and they have a graceful air and engaging deportment. Without the mixture mentioned, the men of rank in Persia, who are descendants of the Tartars (Mongols), would be extremely ugly and deformed."

The Turks have also been much improved in appearance by their intermarriage with the women of Circassia and Georgia, but the system of polygamy has enfeebled the males so that they are, to some extent, a degenerate race.

Dr. Hancock, writing in South America, 1837, says: "The mulattoes, unfortunately and ungenerously held in degradation, are not naturally inferior, I believe, to their fathers, either in moral or physical powers, but certainly far in advance of the primitive African race. * * * It is a well-known fact that the Samboes of South America the progeny of blacks and Indians—are remarkable for their physical superiority over their progenitors of either side."

Dallas observes, in reference to the Maroons in the West India Islands: "They displayed a striking distinction in their personal appearance, being blacker, taller, and, in every respect, handsomer than those on the estate. In their person and carriage, erect, lofty, indicating a consciousness of superiority; vigor appeared in their muscles, and their motions displayed agility. They possessed most, if not all, of the senses in a superior degree."

Prichard says: "If we inquire into the facts which relate to the intermixture of negroes and Europeans, it will be impossible to doubt the tendency of the so-called mulattoes to increase. The men of color, or the mixed race between the Creoles and negroes, are, as in many of the West India Islands, rapidly increasing."

The Cafusos, in Brazil, a mixture of native Americans and negroes, are mentioned by travelers as slender and muscular, and with excessively long hair, which, especially at the end, is half curled, and rises almost perpendicularly from the forehead to the height of a foot or a foot and a half, thus forming a peruke, very beautiful, as a consequence of the mixture of the wool of the negro with the long, stiff hair of the American.

Walker says: "As to the ancient times, we know that some of the greatest men in Greece were of the obscurest origin, and that foreign female slaves gave birth to many of them. A Carian was the mother of Themistecles; a Scythian was that of Demosthenes; and a Thracian gave birth to Iphicrates, and Timotheus."

III.

THE BLENDING OF DIVERSE BLOODS ESSENTIAL TO AMERICAN PROGRESS.

As yet the law governing the rise and fall of races has not been definitely understood. That there is a law operating in all nations, and through all time, is evident to the most casual reader of history. We see races emerge from barbarism, flourish for a hundred or two hundred years, then become degenerate, and relapse into a condition worse than their former barbarism. The law in such cases may be stated thus: It is given to all created things to achieve a certain progress of their own, but a continuance of progress can only be obtained through a judicious crossing of diverse elements. Thus it was given to the Greeks, through a comparatively brief history, to develop a wonderful system of mythology, of philosophy, and of art; to create forms of government that we are to this day experimenting with; then, when ripe with glory, to fall away, to lapse into a semi-barbarism, from which it appears impossible to rescue them. Their history is but the history of all other civilized nations which have succeded them. France, to-day, is in its decline. The Gallic race, originally composed of diverse elements, has been blended into one for so many generations, that the Frenchman is losing in stature, his prolific powers are failing, his intellectual efforts show that finish, polish, precision, and effeminacy, as compared with the rude vigor of nature, which bespeak irreparable decay. The phenomenon has not been generally remarked, that of late years France has become stationary in population; that, in Paris, the number of deaths enormously exceeds the number of births; that the stature of the Frenchman of 1863, is at least three inches shorter than that of the Frenchman of a century since. England maintains its vitality much better. The prolific power of the numerous races which entered into the composition of the modern Englishman has not yet run out, enriched as it is with the Saxon, Celtic, Danish, and other bloods. The Englishman of to-day is of a composite race. The different characteristics (as has been said by a well-known author), may still be seen in different sections of the kingdom. "The Saxon may be found in Norfolk, Suffolk, and Essex, the Celtic in the western highlands, the Danish, with red hair, and the *burr*, in the north of England, the Norwegian further north, the Sclavonic, with cat-like faces, in Carthness." More recently the English people have again intermixed with the Irish and the Scotch. A striking instance of the decay of the races is shown in the history of the Irish. The parts of Ireland that are most habitable, and have the most thrifty population, are those in which Englishmen and Scotchmen have settled. In the north, and other portions of Ireland, the native race, by emigration, and by death, has been steadily decreasing, and will decrease until it blends with a separate people. The Irish, however, transplanted to our soil, become prolific again, because they mix with the American, the German, the Negro, all of whom are brought up under different climatic influences.

But, even the English race itself is beginning to decay. This is shown by the excessive number of females born in that country. They are known to exceed the number of males by over one million. It is a well-known law, that an increase of female population is a symptom of weakness and effeminacy. In the effete races of Northern Mexico, it is remarked that six or seven females are born to one male. The strongest species of animals are those which, like the lion, have a large number of male offspring ; but the weaker animals, such as swine, rabbits, and fowl, have an excessive number of females. It is true of England to-day, and is proved by this and other facts, that its people are losing in vigor.

It is clear that no race can long endure without a commingling of its blood with that of other races. The condition of all human progress is miscegenation. The Anglo-Saxon should learn this in time for his own salvation. If we will not heed the demands of justice, let us, at least, respect the law of self-preservation. Providence has kindly placed on the American soil for his own wise purposes, four millions of colored people. They are our brothers, our sisters. By mingling with them we become powerful, prosperous, and progressive ; by refusing to do so we become feeble, unhealthy, narrow-minded, unfit for the nobler offices of freedom, and certain of early decay.

IV.

THE MARCH OF THE DARK RACES NORTHWARD.

The fact may be startling, but the student of ethnology will be willing to admit that in the course of time the dark races must absorb the white. It is demonstrable from the history of Europe, that the black-haired, black-eyed, swarthy-skinned races have been steadily and surely moving towards northern latitudes.

When Rome was in her pride, the vegetation of Italy, as we learn from the poems of Virgil and Horace, was similar to that which now prevails in Northern Germany and France, and its place has been taken by trees and plants of a more tropical character. The Romans were a lighter people than those which now exist on the shores of the Mediterranean. All the tribes north of the Apennines previous to the time of Cæsar, were yellow-haired, red-bearded—perfect blondes, such as we even now see specimens of in portions of Northern Germany, Sweden, Norway, Denmark, and Scotland. Since that time France has become inhabited almost entirely by brunettes. So, also, has Southern Germany given evidence of a change in the type of its people, in the introduction of traces of the Tartar, in the long, coarse hair, the black eyes, and the yellow skin. England, to-day, is filled with specimens of the darker races. In the olden times the yellow-haired Saxon prevailed over all the British Islands, but he has been conquered by the darker Celt, or changed and improved by the gradual infusion from the South of a richer and more tropical blood. Another thousand years will in all probability see Southern Europe inhabited by a people darker than the Moors, while Northern Europe, in the complexion of its inhabitants, will be similar to the Spain and Italy of to-day.

All the noted ancient and modern wars of Europe may be traced to the yearning of the brunette and blonde to mingle. The Romans conquered the Gauls, Britons, and the Germanic races, to give them the laws and institutions of Rome, and to satisfy this miscegenetic instinct. When Rome fell into decrepitude, the same instinct, as much as the love of plunder and conquest, urged the Hun, Goth, Vandal, and the various tribes of Scythia and Germany, to precipitate themselves upon the plains of southern Europe. Genseric with his yellow-haired Vandals conquered northern Africa to mingle the blood of the two regions. The great wars of modern Europe, including the giant conflicts of Napoleon, have had the effect of intermixing the treasures of different bloods and complexions. Europe is becoming yearly more composite, at least as far as the limit of its races will admit, and consequently more civilized. Thoroughly miscegenetic it cannot be until the Mongolian and African can be brought to its doors.

It will be our noble prerogative to set the example of this rich blending of blood. It is idle to maintain that this present war is not a war for the negro. It is a war for the negro. Not simply for his personal rights or his physical freedom—it is a war if you please, of amalgamation, so called—a war looking, as its final fruit, to the blending of the white and black. All attempts to end it without a recognition of the political, civil, and social rights of the negro will only lead to still bloodier battles in the future. Let us be wise and look to the end. Let the war go on until every black man and every black woman is free. Let it go on until the pride of caste is done away. Let it go on until church, and state, and society recognize not only the propriety but the necessity of the fusion of the white and black—in short, until the great truth shall be declared in our public documents and announced in the messages of our Presidents, that it is desirable the white man should marry the black woman and the white woman the black man—that the race should become melaleuketic before it becomes miscegenetic. The next step will be the opening of California to the teeming millions of eastern Asia. The patience, the industry, the ingenuity, the organizing power, the skill in the mechanic arts, which characterize the Japanese and Chinese, must be transplanted to our soil, not merely by the emigration of the inhabitants of those nations, but by their incorporation with the composite race which will hereafter rule this continent.

It must be remembered that the Indians whom we have displaced were copper-colored, and no other complexion, physiologists affirm, can exist permanently in America. The white race which settled in New England will be unable to maintain its vitality as a blonde people. The darker shades of color live and thrive, and the consumption so prevalent in our Eastern States is mainly confined to the yellow-haired and thin-blooded blondes.

They need the intermingling of the rich tropic temperament of the negro to give warmth and fullness to their natures. They feel the yearning, and do not know how to interpret it. The physician tells them they must travel to a warmer climate. They recognize in this a glimpse of the want they feel, though they are hopeless of its efficacy to fully restore the lost vitality. Still they feel the nameless longing.

"Yet waft me from the harbor mouth,
Wild Wind! I seek a warmer sky,
And I will see before I die
The palms and temples of the South."

It is only by the infusion into their very system of the

vital forces of a tropic race that they may regain health and strength.

We must accept the facts of nature. We must become a yellow-skinned, black-haired people—in fine, we must become Miscegens, if we would attain the fullest results of civilization.

V.

THE MYSTERY OF THE PYRAMIDS—THE SPHYNX QUESTION ANSWERED.

The first instance given us in history of a highly cultivated state of society occurred in a miscegenetic community. We allude to Egypt. As the years roll by and new discoveries are made with regard to this remarkable people, tourists and archæologists are filled with amazement at the evidences of a state of civilization of which even we know nothing. Among the ancient Egyptians the conditions existed for the first time in the history of the world for a high condition of mental culture.

The first requisite is density of population. There must be the collision of mind with mind, and the personal contact of man with man, to intensify the faculties. But, another condition is also necessary. Variety of mental conception is essential to a high development of civilization. The more distant the springs which feed the fountains of knowledge, the richer is the draught supplied to the race. These conditions existed among the Egyptians. The early inhabitants, as has now been discovered, were of a great variety of tribes; some pure black, others red or copper-colored, and others, again, almost white. The ancient Copts, or Quobtes, as

M. Puguet calls them, were a miscegenetic people. Some came from the far south, or equatorial region, and were black and woolly-haired ; others from the deserts of the West, and were copper-colored ; from the East also came a red and yellow tribe, and from the North came the white Thracian or Grecian, all mingling their blood in the ancient Egyptian. Thus ancient historians have given us different accounts of the color of the Egyptians. Herodotus stated that they were black and woolly-haired ; still other Greek writers have said that they were dark colored but with straight hair. Among the mummies are found all varieties except the pure white.

It is clear, therefore, that the Egyptians were a composite race. It was here that civilization dawned, because it was here that the first conditions for civilization existed. The great variety of development of different forms of knowledge brought from distant countries, and better than all, and richer than all, the judicious intermingling of divers tribes from different parts of the earth, produced an intelligent, brave, and progressive people, the like of which has probably never since appeared upon the planet. The arts which have made Greece famous were all undoubtedly of Egyptian origin ; the philosophy that is still discussed in our schools, was first evolved from the miscegenetic mind developed upon the banks of the Nile. As for mechanic arts, it is admitted that with all our discoveries in the physical sciences, with all the marvels effected by steam, we are still far behind the ancient Copts. A pyramid could not be built by any modern people. The immense masses of stone were removed hundreds of miles from their original beds by machinery of which we know nothing. Mr. Wendell Phillips, in his famous lecture on the Lost Arts, shows how many different branches of human industry were known to the ancients, and even to the Egyptians, about which we are entirely ignorant. Even in painting they seem to have possessed a knowledge which the world has lost, for many of the pictures taken from the pyramids are untarnished by time, while those painted bv Titian, Angelo, and Raphael, are chalky and discolored.

The Sphynx question is answered. Egypt calls to us from her tombs, telling us that the secret of progress and of a final perfected humanity lies in the principle of Miscegenation. If we would be raised to the full stature of manhood and womanhood; if we would be as gods, knowing good from evil; if we would fill our proper place in nature, we must mingle our blood with all the children of the common father of humanity. The great lesson of all religions is self-abnegation, the giving up of prejudice, the acknowledgment of our brother man, without regard to his complexion, or creed, or standing, as being dearer to us than our own selves. This is a lesson that America, strong in the pride of color and country, should lay well to heart.

Egypt decayed because her people forgot the lesson their own history should have taught them. After the race became thoroughly composite, they intermarried only with one another, and even carried the breeding in-and-in practice to such an extent that brothers married sisters, and mothers sons. Physical degeneracy and mental imbecility rapidly set in; the nation sank as swiftly as it had soared; and by the operation of the same great law.

VI.

ALL RELIGIONS DERIVED FROM THE DARK RACES.

It is a curious fact that the Caucasian or white race, which of late years has arrogated to itself all the civilization extant, has never yet developed a religious faith of its own. Let the reader peruse any work upon religious creeds and he will find that the whole human family derived their ideas of Deity and of the great hereafter from the earlier and darker races. It is enough to mention Buddhism, Brahmanism, Mahometanism, Judahism, and Christianity, to illustrate our meaning. The Caucasian race, it is true, are intellectual—the perceptive and reasoning organs are large ; yet the sciences upon which we pride ourselves, and the arts which we call our own, are derived primarily from the Asiatics and Africans. Prof. Draper says : "The old white inhabitants of Europe were not able to commence their civilization from their own interior resources, but were thrown into that career by the example and aid of a more southern and darker people, whose climate was more favorable." The white race have originated nothing—they have improved upon many things. They are intellectual, artistic, scientific—in whatever relates to the material they are at home ; but the glories of the Unseen World, the deeper mysteries of the human soul, the relations of humanity to the Omnipotent, the revelations of the hereafter, all there is of aspiration, of religious truth, we learn from the darker Asiatic races ; in short, the whole emotional and spiritual part of our nature is fed by streams from

> "Shiloh's brook, which flows
> Fast by the oracles of God."

Enter a church in any part of Europe or America, and

you will find carefully reproduced the religious creeds of prophets and priests who lived thousands of years ago, in Egypt, Mesopotamia, or the land of the Orient, still further towards the rising sun. All the pure Caucasian race has been able to do has been to invent a cold skepticism, a denial of those religious truths without which the race cannot attain perfection.

May we not hope that in the happier hereafter of this continent, when the Mongolian from China and Japan, and the negro from his own Africa, shall have blent their more emotional natures with ours, that here may be witnessed, at once, the most perfect religion, as well as the most perfect type of mankind the world has yet seen. Let us then embrace our black brother; let us give him the intellect, the energy, the nervous endurance of the cold North which he needs, and let us take from him his emotional power, his love of the spiritual, his delight in the wonders which we understand only through faith. In the beautiful words of Emerson:

"He has the avenues to God
Hid from men of Northern brain,
Far beholding, without cloud,
What these with slowest steps attain."

VII.

THE TYPE MAN A MISCEGEN.

The most recent physiological discoveries have demonstrated that the pale, fair, light hair, mild blue or grey eyes, and sandy, bleached complexions of the blonde or extreme white, are far from being indications of a healthy, refined, and perfected organization. It is among this class that scrofula, consumption, and the nervous diseases prevail. The ideal of the white race—the angels of our painters, the imaginary Christ of our sculptors and artists—is not the perfect ideal of manhood. The true ideal man can only be reached by blending the type man and woman of all the races of the earth. The highest conception of physical beauty possessed by the negro, by the Moor, by the Asiatic, is a model man and woman after their own race ; the negro's Venus is black ; his houris and gods are black ; the divinity of the Hindoo is of the color of his own people ; the Great Spirit of the Indian, if of any color, is copper-colored ; and so through all the world, the highest conception of beauty and perfection is the noblest specimen of each particular community. Humanity's highest type, therefore, is not the white, which comprises only a comparatively small fraction of the people who inhabit the planet.

The ideal or type man of the future will blend in himself all that is passionate and emotional in the darker races, all that is imaginative and spiritual in the Asiatic races, and all that is intellectual and perceptive in the white races. He will also be composite as regards color. The purest Miscegen will be brown, with reddish cheeks, curly and waving hair, dark eyes, and a fullness and suppleness of form not now dreamed of by any individual people. Of course the old races will not be entirely lost sight of. Nature abhors uniformity, and while the highest and purest type will be such as we have described, there will be all shades of color, from white to black. It is to the credit of Professor Draper, of the New York University, that he has had the boldness to avow the physiological fact here announced. He comes to the conclusion, after discussing the question at some length, "That the extremes of humanity, which are represented by a prognathous aspect, and by a complexion either very dark or very fair, are equally unfavorable to intellect, which reaches its greatest perfection in the intermediate phase."

He further says, that "putting disturbances of civilization aside, and looking only to our natural state, we should be constrained to admit that the man of maximum intellectual capacity is of a brown hue."

It is not within the purpose of this book to prove physiological facts ; but simply to state them. They are either true or false. If true, it matters little what critics may say with regard to them; if false, they fall to the ground.

Adam, the progenitor of the race, as his very name signifies, was made of red earth; and, like the inhabitants of Syria and Mesopotamia, must have been of a tawny or yellow color. The extreme white and black are departures from the original type. The Saviour is represented very falsely in paintings, as being light-haired and white-skinned, when, in truth, he must have been a man of very dark complexion, as were all the Palestine Jews. They were a tawny or yellow race. The fact has been noticed that the Amharic, the language of the Abyssinian, is remarkably analogous to the Hebrew, rendering it probable that the Jews were partly of Abyssinian or negro origin.

We urge upon white men and women no longer to glory in their color ; it is no evidence of cultivation or of purity of blood. Adam and Christ, the type men of the world's great eras, were red or yellow, and to men of this color, above all others, must be communicated the higher inspirations which involve great spiritual truths, and which bring individuals of the human family into direct communion with supernatural agencies.

VIII.

LOVE OF THE BLONDE FOR THE BLACK.

Such of our readers as have attended anti-slavery meetings will have observed the large proportion of blondes in the assemblage. This peculiarity is also noticeable in the leading speakers and agitators in the great anti-slavery party. Mr. Horace Greeley, of the New York Tribune, known for his devotion to the negro race, is as opposite as a man possibly can be to the people to whom he has shown his attachment by long and earnest labor for their welfare. In color, complexion, structure, mental habits, peculiarities of all kinds, they are as far apart as the poles. The same is true of Mr. Wendell Phillips. He, too, is the very opposite of the negro. His complexion is reddish and sanguine; his hair in younger days was light; he is, in short, one of the sharpest possible contrasts to the pure negro. Mr. Theodore Tilton, the eloquent young editor of the Independent, who has already achieved immortality by advocating enthusiastically the doctrine of miscegenation, is a very pure specimen of the blonde, and when a young man was noted for his angelic type of feature—we mean angelic after the type of Raphael, which is not the true angelic feature, because the perfect type of the future will be that of the blended races, with the sunny hues of the South tinging the colorless complexion of the icy North. But it is needless further to particularize. The sympathy Mr. Greeley, Mr. Phillips, and Mr. Tilton feel for the negro is the love which the blonde bears for the black; it is a love of race, a sympathy stronger to them than the love they bear to woman. It is founded upon natural law. We love our opposites. It is in the nature of things that we should do so, and where nature has free course, men like those we have indicated, whether anti-slavery or pro-slavery, conservative or radical, democrat or republican, will marry and be given in marriage to the most perfect specimens of the colored race.

It is also remarkable that the anti-slavery agitation is confined to those climates and races that are the furthest removed from the natural home of the colored people. England and the Northern States of North America are strongly anti-slavery. The people of France are also anti-slavery after a fashion, but not so much so as the English. The Spanish people, with their dark hair and skin, have not the love for the negro which distinguishes the more northern races, and hence we never hear of an anti-slavery propaganda on the Spanish peninsula. The further south we go the less the sympathy for the negro ; the further north, the greater.

Nor is it alone true that the blonde love the black. The black also love their opposites. Said Frederick Douglass, a noble specimen of the melaleuketic American, in one of his speeches : "We love the white man, and will remain with him. We like him too well to leave him ; but we must possess with him the rights of freemen." Our police courts give painful evidence that the passion of the colored race for the white is often so uncontrollable as to over come the terror of the law. It has been so, too, upon the southern plantations. The only remedy for this is legitimate melaleuketic marriage. As Novalis wisely says : "The way to overcome nature, is to submit to her."

It is true that a few men of dark skin, and eyes, and hair are to be found among the anti-slavery leaders ; but it will be remarked by any careful observer that it is not so much the love of the negro that animates these men as hatred of the slaveholder. The case of Owen Lovejoy is one in point. He hates the South because the slaveholders murdered his brother. The bitterness manifested by these dark-skinned, dark-haired, dark eyed, saturnine northern men towards the southern man is due to the strong antipathy and opposition which always exists between males of a kindred type ; but if the southern woman was a blonde, golden-haired, blue-eyed, and of sunny complexion, they would love her. The law therefore is that we love our opposites. Walker, in his work on Intermarriage, says: "In the vital systems the dry seek the humid ; the meagre, the plump ; the hard, the softer ; the rough, the smoother ; the warmer, the colder ; the dark, the fairer, &c., upon the same principles. * * * In the mental system, the irritable seek the calm ; the grave, the gay ; the impassioned, the modest ; the impetuous, the gentle, &c. ; or in opposite cases the opposite. In all this it is not what we possess ourselves, it is something different, something new, something capable of exciting, which is sought for, and this conforms to the fundamental difference of the sexes."

IX.

PRESENT AND FUTURE OF THE IRISH AND THE NEGRO.

Notwithstanding the apparent antagonism which exists between the Irish and negroes on this continent, there are the strongest reasons for believing that the first movement towards a melaleuketic union will take place between these two races. Indeed, in very many instances it has already occurred. Wherever there is a poor community of Irish in the North, they naturally herd with the poor negroes, and as the result of the various offices of kindness which only the poor pay to one another, families become intermingled and connubial relations are formed between the black men and white Irish women. These matrimonial arrangements have generally been pleasant to both parties, and were it not for the unhappy prejudice which exists, such unions would be very much more frequent. The white Irishwoman loves the black man, and in the old country, it has been stated, that the negro, is sure of the handsomest among the poor white females. The very bitterness of feeling which exists on the part of the Irish in the large cities towards the negroes is an evidence that they will be the first to mingle. The disturbances created when brought into contact present the same phenomena as the attempted fusion of kindred electricities—repugnance and flying apart are followed by the closest of all unions. The fusion, whenever it takes place, will be of infinite service to the Irish. They are a more brutal race and lower in civilization than the negro. The latter is mild, spiritual, fond of melody and song, warm in his attachments, fervid in his passions, but inoffensive and kind, and only apparently brutal when his warmest emotions are brought into play in his love for the white woman. The Irish are coarse-grained, revengeful, unintellectual, with very few of the finer instincts of humanity. Of course we speak of the laboring Irish as they appear in this country. The Milesian is a child of the sun. He was originally of a colored race, and has all the fervid emotional power which belongs to a people born in or near the tropics. His long habitation north, however, and the ignorance in which he has been kept by misgovernment, have sunk the Irishman below the level of the most degraded negro. Take an equal number of negroes and Irish from among the lowest communities of the city of New York, and the former will be found far superior to the latter in cleanliness, education, moral feelings, beauty of form and feature, and natural sense. One of the evidences of degeneracy which has been pointed out in certain of the negro races has been the prognathous skull, the projecting mouth, the flat and open nostril. Yet this is a characteristic as true of certain portions of the people of Ireland as of the Guinea African. The inhabitants of Sligo and Mayo, portions of Ireland under peculiarly bad government, have developed these precise types of feature. The people have become thin-legged, pot-bellied, with mouth projected, head sloped, nostril distended ; in short they exhibit all the characteristics by which we have marked the lowest type of the negro. The blending of the Irish in this country with the negro will be a positive gain to the former. With education and an intermingling with the superior black, the Irish may be lifted up to something like the dignity of their ancestors, the Milesians. The poets who sang of the ancient Irish, of the wisdom of their rulers, of their bards and warriors, forgot, perhaps, that this noble old race was of a very dark complexion, and native of the far south. The red hair and beard so common in Ireland is a sure indication of the southern origin of its people. When a very dark people move to a northern climate the physiological change effected by the temperature is to convert the black into red hair. The red may change in the course of many generations into light or sandy, but the red which comes from a very dark people is not to be confounded with the blonde or light-brown which distinguishes a northern people.

The Irish-American press of this country have a duty to perform to their patrons in impressing these facts upon our Irish population. The black man is their brother in more senses than one, and, as in times past the Irish have shown themselves the most prejudiced and inhuman toward their dark-skinned fellow-laborers and friend, they should in the future set aside the prejudice which is the result of unfortunate education, and proclaim, both by word and by the practice of intermarriage, their true relations with the negro.

X.

THE MISTAKE OF ALL RELIGIONS AND SYSTEMS OF EDUCATION.

Let the author here announce a law which has been overlooked by all past reformers—a law vital in itself, and accounting for the inadequacy of religion and education to perfect the races of men.

Education and religious instruction must come to us through the roots of our being—through the springs of our life. They are ante-natal, and are to be imparted before the child is born—before the man is matured. The error of all religion and education has been in appealing to the higher faculties, and ignoring the influence of the lower. After the product of purely physical causes is matured, the ministers and teachers take the child in hand and attempt to change the organic bias of his nature by appeals to his intellectual and moral faculties. He is sent to the church and to the Sunday-school to receive an infusion of religion. Veneration, hope, fear, credulity, fancy, are appealed to; but behind all these sentiments, and behind the reasoning faculties, lie the great normal powers of our being, which neither ministers nor teachers can recreate. It is as if the gardener should undertake to change the character of the plant after it has attained its growth. It is as if he should attempt to alter the fruit of the tree through its leaves, instead of through its roots. The whole theory is wrong. We are the children of our ancestors. The moral and physical characteristics of the parents are "visited upon the children to the third and fourth generation." We are moulded in the forms of their passions. So nations, that keep themselves exclusive, are limited to the narrow range of faculties possessed by their ancestors. The stream cannot rise higher than its source.

It may be objected, that this is a material view of our condition. But we are material beings. The sources of our life, as of the trees of the forest, are in the earth. If planted rightly, the tree will grow strong and shapely; if planted wrongly, or under unfavorable circumstances, it will grow gnarled, crooked, and dwarfed; and after the mischief is once accomplished, neither care or cultivation can give it any other character. So, religion and education cannot make a man what he should be, if his whole being has been depraved by ante-natal influences. Let it be understood, then, that

1st. The perfection of the race can be achieved only by proper attention to all the conditions which go to make up superior men and women, mentally and physically.

2d. All education which instructs from the top downward is wrong: men, like plants, must be developed from the roots upwards.

Let the friends of humanity, then, uuderstand that it is not by forwarding religious and educational institutions alone that they can bring about the Millenium.

Churches and universities fill, of course, their appropriate spheres in ministering to the intellectual and moral wants of the race, but there are other, and apparently grosser agencies which will prove more effectual in ushering in the millenial man and woman. This, however, is not a matter to be discussed at length in these pages. Science will yet deliver the human race from all the bonds which cramp its powers. The veil of that awful mystery cannot as yet be raised.

XI.

HOW THE ANGLO-AMERICAN MAY BECOME STRONG AND COMELY.

The white people of America are dying for want of flesh and blood. They have bone and sinew, but they are dry and shriveled for lack of the healthful juices of life. The author has often sadly marked the contrast to to be observed in social or intellectual gatherings of the negro and the white American. In the latter are seen unmistakably, the indications of physical decay. The cheeks are shrunken, the lips are thin and bloodless, the under jaw narrow and retreating, the teeth decayed and painful, the nose sharp and cold, the eyes small and watery, the complexion of a blue and yellow hue, the head and shoulders bent forward, the hair dry and straggling upon the men, the waists of the women thin and pinched, telling of sterility and consumption, the general appearance gaunt and cadaverous from head to foot. You will see bald heads upon young men. You will see eye-glasses and spectacles, false teeth, artificial color in the face, artificial plumpness to the form. The intercourse will be formal, ascetic, unemotional. You will see these characteristics so universal that they become rather the rule than the exception. Where the cheeks on one grown person will be rounded, and tinted with the healthy blood, ten persons will have them pale and hollow. Turn now to an assemblage of negroes. Every cheek is plump ; the teeth are whiter than ivory ; there are no bald heads, the eyes are large and bright, the head and shoulders are always up and back, every face wears a smile, every form is stalwart. The white man is going to seed ; the black man is adding vigor and freshness to the trunk. The white child is born with full cheeks, but as he approaches manhood they fall away and are lank and thin. Nature did not intend that men's cheeks should be hollow. The dentists' signs in every locality only tell feebly of the sickness and racking pain that accompanies this weak and diseased condition of the jaws. Our professional men show more than any the lack of healthful association with their opposites of the other sex. They become thin, and gaunt, and old, when they should be strong and vigorous. They are told they need exercise ; they take long walks in the morning air, and come back more cold and shriveled than ever. They need contact with healthy, loving, warm-blooded natures to fill up the lean interstices of their anatomy. Looking purely to physical benefits for themselves and their posterity, they might well form the resolve expressed in Tennyson's lines :

> " I will take some savage woman ; she shall rear my dusky race ;
> Iron-jointed, supple-sinewed, they shall dance and they shall run,
> Catch the wild goat by the hair, and hurl their lances in the sun ;
> Whistle back the parrot's call, and leap the rainbows of the brooks,
> Not with blinded eyesight poring over miserable books."

XII.

THE MISCEGENETIC IDEAL OF BEAUTY IN WOMAN.

In what does beauty consist? In richness and brightness of color, and in gracefulness of curve and outline. What does the Anglo-Saxon, who assumes that his race monopolizes the beauty of the earth, look for in a lovely woman? Her cheeks must be rounded, and have a tint of the sun, her lips must be pouting, her teeth white and regular, her eyes large and bright; her hair must curl about her head, or descend in crinkling waves; she must be merry, gay, full of poetry and sentiment, fond of song, childlike and artless. But all these characteristics belong, in a somewhat exaggerated degree, to the negro girl. What color is beautiful in the human face? Is it the blank white? In paintings, the artist has never portrayed so perfect a woman to the fancy, as when choosing his subject from some other than the Caucasian race, he has been able to introduce the marvelous charm of the combination of colors in her face. Not alone to the white face, even when tinted with mantling blood, is the fascination of female loveliness imputed. The author may state—and the same experience can be witnessed to by thousands—that the most beautiful girl in form, feature, and every attribute of feminine loveliness he ever saw, was a mulatto. By crossing and improvement of different varieties, the strawberry, or other garden fruit, is brought nearest to perfection, in sweetness, size, and fruitfulness. This was a ripe and complete woman, possessing the best elements of two sources of parentage. Her complexion was warm and dark, and golden with the heat of tropical suns, lips full and luscious, cheeks perfectly moulded, and tinged with deep crimson, hair curling, and

> "Whose glossy black
> To shame might bring
> The plumage of the raven's wing."

For certain physiological reasons, the mulattoes of this country are far from being true specimens of the results of miscegnetic reform; but occasionally there are combinations of circumstances which produce the superior of either of the parents. The "happy mean" between the physical characteristics of the white and black, forms the nearest approach to the perfect type of beauty in womanhood, and of strength and wisdom in manhood. The model of nature, will be one possessing in even balance all the characteristics of the various nations of the earth. Shakespeare, who said many things that in the light of after events seem almost prophetic, described briefly and completely the model representative of humanity:

> "The elements
> So mixed in him that nature might stand up,
> And say to all the world, 'This was a man.'"

Descriptions by travelers, of the beauty of negro and colored women, and of the stalwart and fine proportions of negro men, might be given here at length. It is sufficient that the colored girl may appear very beautiful in the eye of the white man. Adanson says of the negroes of Senegal: "Leur taille est pour l'ordinaire, au dessus de la mediocre, bien prise et sans défaut. Ils sont forts, robustes, et d'un temperament propre à la fatigue. Ils ont les traits du visage assez agreables." Of the women he says: "Leur visage est d'une douceur extrême. Elles ont yeux noirs bien fendus, la bouche et les lèvres petites et les traits du visage bien proportionnées. Il s'en trouve plusieurs d'une beauté parfaite."

Reynolds says, of the abstract question of beauty: "It is custom alone determines our preference of the color of the Europeans to the Ethiopians, and they, for the same reason, prefer their own color to ours. I suppose nobody will doubt, if one of their painters were to paint the Goddess of Beauty, but that he would represent her black, with thick lips, flat nose, and woolly hair; and it seems to me he would act very unnaturally if he did not, for by what criterion will any one dispute the propriety of his idea? We, indeed, say that the form and color of the European is preferable to that of the Ethiopian, but I know of no other reason we have for it, but that we are more accustomed to it."

He might have said that the criterion to beauty is the medium between all distinct models, and that such a criterion all the world would acknowledge.

Payne Knight says: "The sable Africans view with pity and contempt, the marked deformity of the Europeans, whose mouths are compressed, their noses pinched, their cheeks shrunk, their hair rendered lank and flimsy, their bodies lengthened and emaciated, and their skin unnaturally bleached by shade and seclusion, and the baneful influence of a cold, humid climate." These prejudices of the African against the European, are well-founded, but this is no reason why they should look upon us with "pity and contempt." For we have also our superiorities over the African, mostly intellectual, and these unnatural prejudices which destroy in the heart the sacred emotions of brotherhood, are the ruin of the races. There is in each race those elements which are needed to supply the deficiencies of the other. But these prejudices are dying out, and nature is asserting again the unity of all men. The negro now declares that he loves the white man, and the progressive party of the North assert the rights of the negro. The leaders of Progress—among whom we quote Phillips and Tilton—urge miscegenetic reform. The people are ripe to receive the truth. Through the fiery gate of war they are being led to deliverance from old prides and prejudices. And, indeed, the instinct of the white man responded to the call of the negro for fraternity. There were wants in his nature which only the negro could fill. There were defects in physical organization that only the negro could supply. There were cravings of the soul toward fraternity, that only the negro could comfort and satisfy. It is a mean pride, unworthy of a Christian or enlightened community, that should lead any to deny this. The success of the anti-slavery party has proved it, so that denial of the principle is denial of facts universally known. They have touched a chord that has vibrated with a sweet, strange, and marvelous music, awakening slumbering instincts in the heart of the nation and of the world. It has been felt alike by the free and the enslaved. When a deed is done for freedom and brotherhood, in the grand words of James Russell Lowell:

"Through the earth's broad, aching breast,
Runs a thrill of joy prophetic, trembling on from East to West,
And the slave, where'er he cowers, feels the soul within him climb
To the awful verge of manhood, as the energy sublime
Of a century, bursts full blossomed on the thorny stem of time.

Through the walls of hut and palace shoots the instantaneous throe,
When the travail of the Ages wrings earth's systems to and fro;
At the birth of each new Era, with a recognizing start,
Nation wildly looks on nation, standing with mute lips apart,
And glad truth's yet mightier man-child, leaps beneath the future's heart.

For mankind are one in spirit, and an instinct bears along,
Round the earth's electric circle, the swift flash of right or wrong,
Whether conscious or unconscious, yet humanity's vast frame,
Through its ocean-sundered fibers, feels the gush of joy or shame;
In the gain or loss of *one* race, *all the rest* have equal claim."

XIII.

THE SECRET OF SOUTHERN SUCCESS.

The North is wondering—the world is wondering—at the marvelous success of the Southern people in statesmanship and war. The discretion, endurance, energy, and heroism they have shown in sustaining for so long a time a rebellion supposed to be feeble and short-lived, have elicited the admiration even of their enemies ; and Dr. Bellows, a gentleman than whom none can claim a more exalted and intense hate of slavery and of the rebellion, in an address before a Unitarian assemblage in Brooklyn, some time ago, paid a most eloquent and beautiful tribute to Southern chivalry, both as exhibited in the men and women. The truth may as well be understood, that the superiority of the slaveholding classes of the South arises from their intimate communication, from birth to death, with the colored race. Like Anteus, sent to his mother earth, they have risen reinvigorated The unnatural separation of races which exists at the North, and the prejudice which keeps the poor whites of the South from the slave, have prevented a large portion of the American people from profiting by the presence of the negro in our midst. When this war opened, one of the leading English Reviews (the Edinburgh) had an article proving that the governing class at the South were superior men physically to those of the North; and it is true. The comments of the Northern press respecting the inferiority of the Southerners were true of the poor whites—of the sand-hillers and corncrackers, so well described in Mrs. Stowe's novels. But these people are kept apart, by their unwholesome prejudices, from the negro. Because they cannot mingle with him in the capacity of slaveholder, they shut themselves up in their unnatural pride, and shun the race that, even in its enslaved condition, is their superior. Their exclusiveness has been punished by their own physical inferiority. But it is otherwise with the so-called aristocratic classes of the South. The most intimate association exists. But the instinct here becomes a passion, and is often shameful and criminal.

On this point we might quote many pro and anti-slavery authorities, but the extracts would scarcely be fit for general reading. It is a notorious fact, however, that, for three generations back, the wealthy, educated, governing class of the South have mingled their blood with the enslaved race. These illicit unions, though sanctioned neither by law nor conscience, and which, therefore, are degrading morally, have helped to strengthen the vitality and add to the mental force of the Southerner. The emotional power, fervid oratory and intensity which distinguishes all thoroughbred slaveholders, is due to their intimate association with the most charming and intelligent of their slave girls. The local history of New Orleans, since its occupation by the Union army, proves what has often been suspected, that unions between the slaveholders and their slaves have often had, in the eyes of the parties themselves, all the sanctities of marriage. These facts give us an inkling of some of the sources of Southern power. The vigor to be derived from the contact with another race has never before been explained, because never suspected.

The idea that the Southerner has been benefited by his association with the black man is thus set forth, in a speech made by the Hon. Seth B. Cole, at a meeting of a Loyal League Club in Brooklyn. It will be found reported in the Brooklyn *Eagle*, of June 20th, 1863 :

" In accounting for the ability of the South successfully to cope with Union men, and maintain a persistence in the Cabinet, in battle, and on the sea, foreign to their character, and worthy of a better cause, the gentleman gave it as his belief, that the presence of the

African in large numbers infused into the air a sort of barbaric malaria, a miasm of fierceness which, after long intercourse between the races, came to infect the white men and even the women also. On the contrary, the inferior race was made smoother, more, polished, and toned down by association with the superior. On this principle, therefore, he accounted for the wild, chivalrous spirit of the South; this combination of wild poison with the polish of the Southron made them great in many respects, and infusing itself into all grades of society, enabled the rebels for a time to overcome, or at least fairly contest with, their Northern opponents. The realization of the fact, that this fierceness and fiery wildness of the negro was the real cause of the frequent success of Southern strategy and campaigning came slow, but the speaker thanked God that at last the nation understood it, and was already availing itself of it by putting the Africans, with all these traits developed, in the field against their most polished imitation. The black regiments in the field, and others to go, could compete with the wildness and recklessness of the rebels, and possessing this barbaric miasma in a greater degree could defeat them."

XIV.

HEART-HISTORIES OF THE WHITE DAUGHTERS OF THE SOUTH.

Nor are the Southern women indifferent to the strange magnetism of association with a tropical race. Far otherwise. The mothers and daughters of the aristocratic slaveholders are thrilled with a strange delight by daily contact with their dusky male servitors. These relations, though intimate and full of a rare charm to the passionate and impressible daughters of the South, seldom, if ever, pass beyond the bounds of propriety. A platonic love, a union of sympathies, emotions, and thoughts, may be the sweetness and grace of a woman's life, and without any formal human tie, may make her thoroughly happy.

And this is the secret of the strange infatuation of the Southern woman with the hideous barbarism of slavery. Freedom, she knows, would separate her forever from the colored man, while slavery retains him by her side. It is idle for the Southern woman to deny it; she loves the black man, and the raiment she clothes herself with is to please him. What are the distinguishing characteristics of a Southern woman's attire? Why, bright colors—a tendency to yellow and pale red, and those striking gold ornaments which make such a charming contrast to a dark skin, but are so out of place in the toilet of a blonde. Yes—the Southern beauty, as she parades her bright dresses and inappropriate colors in our Northern cities and watering-places, proclaims by every massive ornament in her shining hair, and by every yellow shade in the wavy folds of her dress, "I love the black man."

Nor, in view of the powerful attraction of the two, races, is this frenzy of love in the white Southern woman for the negro, altogether inexplicable. The family is isolated on the plantations. The white young man is away at college, traveling in Europe, or practicing at his profession in the large cities, while the white girl, who matures early, is at her home, surrounded by the brightest and most intelligent of the young colored men on the estate. Passionate, full of sensibility, without the cold prudence of her Northern sister, who can wonder at the wild dreams of love which fire the hearts and fill the imagination of the impressible Southern maiden. The awkward, rude girl of yesterday, under the influence of the master passion of our common humanity, is changed in a day to the full measure of a glorious womanhood.

It is safe to say that the first heart experience of nearly every Southern maiden—the flowering sweetness and grace of her young life, is associated with a sad dream of some bondman lover. He may have been the waiter, or coachman, or the bright yellow lad who assisted the overseer; but to her he is a hero, blazing with all the splendors of imperial manhood. She treasures the looks from those dark eyes which made her pulses bound; every spot of earth, where he had awaited her coming, is, to her, holy ground.

The first bitter lesson of a woman's life—self-sacrifice—they learn when prejudice and pride of caste compels them to tear the loved image from their hearts. What wondrous romances are yet to be written on this sad but charming theme; what wealth of passional life is lost with all the heart-histories of the South blotted out by a blighting prejudice—a cruel pride of caste and color. The full mystery of sex—the sweet, wild dream of a perfect love, which will embrace all that is fervid and emotional in humanity, can never be generally known until men and women the world over are free to form unions with their opposites in color and race. The rule in love affinities is the same as in electrical affinities: unlike attract—like repel.

But while estimating the influence of the black upon the white race, we must not overlook the reverse action. The black race is also beneficially affected even when there is no intermarriage. On this point Dr. Hancock, the American traveler, says: "It has appeared to me that various obvious changes are produced in a few generations, from certain assimilations independently of intermarriage. We find, in negro families, which have long dwelt with those of the whites as domestics, that successive generations become less marked in their African features, in the thick lip and flat nose; and with skins of a shining black, they gradually acquire the European physiognomy."

XV.

ALL OUR VICTORIOUS BATTLE-FIELDS BAPTIZED BY THE BLOOD OF THE NEGRO.

Napoleon said of his battles, that Providence fought on the side which had the most cannon, but it is manifest from the history of the campaigns of the present civil war, that Heaven fights on the side of the armies which make use of the greatest number of negroes. Heaven never smiled upon our cause until the issuance of the Proclamation of Freedom, nor even then until it was determined to arm the negro in defense of his own liberty. It is a remarkable fact—we wish to impress it upon all who consider this subject—that wherever the negro has been used as a soldier in our armies, there, and only there, have we been successful. Our great victories in the West, are all of them associated with the valor of colored soldiers. Except at Donelson, there is not a battle-field of any consequence, from the Alleghanies to the borders of Texas, that has not traces of the blood of the negro soldier. They fought at Milliken's Bend, pending the attack on Vicksburg; their blood glorified the soil below the ramparts of Port Hudson; Grant and Banks, who recognized the negro soldier, are always victorious; Rosecrans who armed the negro, but refused to fight with him, was only partially successful; while the Army of the Potomac which would never tolerate a negro soldier in its ranks has invariably been defeated, except in a defensive battle, and upon its own soil. Whatever measure of success attends the operations against Charleston will be due to the negroes employed ; and if we are not entirely successful it is because Gen. Gilmore's prejudices lead him to keep the best and bravest troops in the trenches, instead of in the field. The author does not claim that the negro is necessarily a better soldier than the white man, though he is quite as good, but does assert that there is a providence in the solution of the question of race on this continent. It can be solved only by showing that the colored man, despised, down-trodden, contemned, is yet to be the savior of the nation. It has been so ordained. Charles Sumner eloquently says :

"Wherever I turn in this war I find the African. If you ask for strategy, I know nothing better than that of the slave Robert Small, who brought the rebel steamer Planter, with its armament, out of Charleston, and surrendered it to our Commodore as a prize of war. If you ask for successful courage, I know nothing better than that of the African Tillman, who rose upon a rebel prize crew, and overcoming them, carried the ship into New York. If you ask for heroism, you will find it in that nameless African, on board the Pawnee, who, while passing shell from the magazine, lost both his legs by a ball, but still holding the shell, cries out : 'Pass up the shell, never mind me, my time is up.' And if you ask for fidelity you will find it in that slave, also without a name, who pointed out the road of safety to the harassed, retreating Army of the Potomac. And if you ask for evidence of the desire for freedom, you will find it in the little slave girl, journeying North, whom Banks took on his cannon."

In view of these facts, patent to all who have studied the history of the civil war, and to none more than the soldiers in the field, we urge upon them to do justice to their fellow colored soldiers. In the words of Boker, in his spirited lyric to the remains of the regiment which fought so gallantly at Port Hudson:

> O, to the living few,
> Soldiers, be just and true!
> Hail them as comrades tried:
> Fight with them side by side:
> Never, in field or tent,
> Scorn the black regiment!

The author cannot refrain, in this connection, from quoting the following passage from Mr. Emerson's new poem, entitled, "Voluntaries":

> Freedom all winged expands,
> Nor perches in a narrow place,
> Her broad van seeks implanted lands,
> She loves a poor and virtuous race.
> Clinging to the colder zone
> Whose dark sky sheds the snow-flake down,
> The snow-flake is her banner's star,
> Her stripes the boreal streamers are.
> Long she loved the Northmen well;
> Now the iron age is done,
> She will not refuse to dwell
> With the offspring of the sun,
> Foundling on the desert far,
> Where palms plume and siroccos blaze,
> He roves unhurt the burning ways
> In climates of the summer star.
> He has avenues to God
> Hid from men of Northern brain,
> Far beholding, without cloud,
> What these with slowest steps attain.
> If once the generous chief arrive
> To lead him, willing to be led,
> For Freedom he will strike and strive,
> And drain his heart till he be dead.

XVI.

PROGRESS OF PUBLIC OPINION AND NATIONAL POLICY TOWARDS MISCEGENATION.

The right of the negro to be free is now almost universally acknowledged. It is only those who are actuated by the meanest motives of personal interest who attempt to question it. The equality of the race is acknowledged far and wide. Its superiority in many of those characteristics which enter into the beau ideal of true manhood, is unquestionable. The necessity of the mingling of the race with ours as the only means of preserving us from the decay that inevitably follows the highest state of enlightenment and exclusiveness is beginning to be understood. The truth is dawning upon us. The light that glimmers along the horizon will soon break all over the sky.

In this war there has been seen the working of a marvellous Providence, The prejudices of many generations have been swept away in the tide of events. When we come to the dry land again we shall find ourselves across an ocean misty and stormy with old bigotries, superstitions, and passions. Let us pray that we rest our feet on no shoals or quicksands of compromise; but never cease our struggle, having saved this persecuted race from the waters, until we stand with them on the broad and solid ground of justice, equality, and fraternity.

No party in this country has yet dared, openly and unanimously, to speak the truth. But the times are big with hope. We see one party battling for the slave and another against him. We see in the North one party casting aside old prejudices; we see another clinging to them. It is only a question now when all will loose their hold. But we see progress more distinctly not in the defeat of one party by the other, so much as in the higher ground which both occupy. One presses forward and the other must follow it even to fight it. Yet the one the most advanced has not reached the *ultima thule* of its theories. Four years ago the Democrats, so-called, defended slavery, and the Republicans only dared to assert an opposition to the extension of slavery. The Republican party to-day boldly demands that every black man in the land shall be free; that he shall stand side by side with the white soldier in the defense of liberty and law; that the plantations of the South shall be transferred to him from his rebel master; that by the Government and people his services shall be recognized; that he shall receive from the white North the right hand of fellowship as the reward of his loyalty. The Democratic party hardly dares to oppose all this, but attempts to divert discussion to senseless side issues, such as peace, free speech, and personal and constitutional rights. In the olden time the master said, as loyal men say to-day, "He that is not with me is against me." When he cast out devils, as Burnside did in Ohio, and went about doing good as opportunity offered, to the poor and the oppressed, the hypocrites were horrified, and talked to him of the law and of the prophets, as the traitors of to-day talk of courts and constitutions. It is fitting that we should brand these men with the name of Copperheads, remembering how he addressed his audience of cavilers and hypocrites: "O! generation of vipers!"

The position of the Republican party to-day proves how far we are toward the truth. We have been driven. We have been carried in a whirlwind. It would have taken a thousand years in the old way to have come to this. But the party will not perform its whole mission till it throws aloft the standard of (so-called) Amalgamation. When the President proclaimed Emancipation he proclaimed also the mingling of the races. The one follows the other as surely as noonday follows sunrise. The party, as a whole, will not admit it yet. They move in the darkness, not knowing what the day will reveal to them. They denied that they were abolitionists. It was only at the commencement of this war that Congress, in its infinite stupidity, resolved that "neither the Federal Government, nor the people, nor the Governments of the non-slaveholding States have a purpose or constitutional right to legislate upon or interfere with slavery," and "that those persons in the North who do not subscribe to the foregoing proposition are too insignificant in numbers and influence to excite the serious attention or alarm of any portion of the people of the Republic, and that the increase of their numbers and influence does not keep pace with the increase of the aggregate population of the Union." They were all conservatives then! But they had set their faces towards the light; they could not stand still; they could not go backward. And now, behold! the great Republican party has merged into the little abolition party. The drop has colored the bucket-full. There are only two parties now, the Abolition, which is, in effect, the party of miscegenation; and, behind them, that contemptible crowd who fear the South, and have no policy for the North but expediency Why did abolitionism swallow Republicanism? Because it was founded on principles that approach nearer the truth. Because one man who is right is a majority against the world.

The people do not yet understand; but the old prejudices are being swept away. They say we must free the negroes. To free them is to recognize their equality with the white man. They are to compete with the white man in all spheres of labor. They are to receive wages. They are to provide for themselves. Therefore they will have the opportunity to rise to wealth and high position. Said a speaker at a Republican meeting at the Cooper Institute, in New York: "If the time ever comes when a majority of the people of this State desire a negro Governor, and elect him as such, I believe he ought to be Governor." It was a statement that commended itself to the common sense of the audience, and they did well to applaud. And the argument goes further. If a white woman shall prefer this black Governor, or any black man of wealth or distinction, for her husband, rather than an ignorant or drunken white man, she certainly ought to have him.

They dare to assert now, too, that the black man should be allowed to fight for us, maintaining that he will fight as well as the white man. So he will. If he may fight to protect our homes and firesides, why may he not enjoy a cordial association in our families and social circles? Shall the fair, whose smiles are the proverbial reward of bravery, discriminate as to color where merit is equal? The war is doing good in this, that our soldiers are mingling with the blacks now, as the whites of the south have mingled with them. But the association is more ennobling, because the black is now free, and may become, by industry and self-improvement, the equal of the white intellectually, as he is now physically and morally. The blacks that move with our regiments are beloved by their comrades; they perform the most valuable duties in the field—duties requiring courage and sagacity, with greater success than the white soldiers. There is a darker side to this picture which should be its brightest. The loves that have sprung up between the freed women and our soldiers have only been hinted at in public, though known by those who have followed our armies into slave regions to be universal and inevitable. The vacuum in the soldier's nature draws into itself the strength and the womanly fullness of the ripe and beautiful dark-skinned girl. The yearning instinct is satisfied at last, despite long-settled prejudices and blasphemous theories.

It is boldly announced now that the lands of rebel whites should be confiscated, and given to loyal negroes, in part payment of the debt of the nation toward them. They will then be peers in the land, able to educate and improve themselves. It is not contended here that the highly cultivated of any class should marry with the degraded. The elegant and refined gentleman would not find a congenial companion in the dirty, ignorant, and misformed Irish girl from the emigrant ships ; the victim of poverty and despotism. So the influence of slavery must have been, in many instances, to degrade the negro far below his own standard in all the better attributes of man, and thus to render him unfit for marriage with the better classes. But there is an ideal of physical superiority to be found among the negro girls of the South that would give the incitement of warm and v gorous health to the chilly-blooded effeminacy that too often accompanies education and talent. The aristocrat of the South, for a century has gained strength by the association with his slaves. Let the poor and degraded whites of the South mingle with the negroes who have also partaken of the bitter fruits of slavery ; let our soldiers occupy the plantations with those that are more fitted for their companionship, and the next generation will be a people worthy to occupy the sunny land that God has laid out there—a people who shall—

"Walk in beauty like the night
Of cloudless climes and starry skies,
And all that's best of dark and bright,
Meet in their aspect and their eyes"

Public opinion now acknowledges that the North is much to blame for slavery, because of the prejudice against the negro. But how is this prejudice to be removed? A separate race is always hated. The Jews have been the scoff and by-word of nations, simply because they were exclusive. The negro can only be respected and loved when he mingles with us, and becomes one of the elements of our race. The colonization scheme of the President has fallen stillborn from his pen. There was none so poor to do it reverence, but Montgomery Blair. And the illogical, mean, and blasphemous speech which that man made at the capital of New Hampshire in June, 1863, has been sufficiently castigated by Wendell Phillips. The Republican party now wisely admits that we must let the negro remain with us, recognizing him as one of the great elements of our strength and prosperity. We have quoted the remark of Frederick Douglass concerning the love of the negro for the white. But it would be better for him to be transported to some foreign shore, to linger in poverty, and die in wretchedness, than to remain here isolated by prejudice from the white, persecuted, and hated. It has been the question always with the opponents of justice, "What will you do with the negro when he is free?" This is the answer, and the only answer: "We will take him into our societies, into our churches, into our schools, into our social circles, into our families; we will receive him as our younger brother." The Abolitionists did not answer thus in words; but their practice led to the true answer. They did not know, perhaps, the impulse that moved them. It was the sympathetic surging of the great heart of humanity towards the negro. As nature reveals the long-lost child to its mother, so the human heart went out towards its brother. It was a longing towards the realization of the common brotherhood, of the unity of the nations, which are the promise of all morality and of all Christianity. Might we hope that on this continent, at least, will be realized the vision of Tennyson :

"Far along the world-wide whisper of the Southwind rushing warm,
With the standards of the peoples plunging through the thunder storm,
Till the war-drums throbbed no longer, and the battle-flags were furl'd
In the Parliament of man ; the Federation of the world.
There the common sense of most, shall hold a fretful realm in awe ;
And the kindly earth shall slumber, lapt in universal law."

XVII.

THE BLOODS OF ALL NATIONS FIND THEIR LEVEL.

Whatever men may do, the immutable laws of nature are not subverted through the ages. For a brief period here, for a generation there, the great principles of equality may be ignored, and men may suffer. But not always. Man, though bent to the earth, surely becomes upright again. He holds in his hands the eternal years of God.

"Through the ages one increasing purpose runs,
And the thoughts of men are widened
With the process of the suns"

You may build cisterns, and canals, and levees ; but some time, the water that you seek to confine will find its level again. Not the less so with the blood of man. As God made of one blood all nations of the earth, and as all are brothers from Adam ; so, whatever artificial distinctions and barriers men may raise, the blood of humanity will at the end find its certain level.

There are nations that have built walls about themselves, as it were, so that their blood should not flow out, nor the blood of the nations outside flow in. They have said, "We will purify, and sweeten, and enrich the treasure of our veins. We will fill this nation full to the brim with gentle and noble blood, but will never let it overflow. And we will walk about on the turrets of our outside walls, and look upon all the other people of the earth, cold and lean below us." They denied the brotherhood of man ; they failed to see the stamp of God on every brow. But the blood so confined became stagnant and fermented, so that before a century had passed it burst the bounds and ran out with wild force to mingle with that of barbarians outside. And the walls were torn down and again humanity was leveled. There are families that have hoarded their blood, as the miser his gold ; and, as the gold cankers, so the blood has grown thick and muddy, losing its elements of health and vigor, and has only been rescued from death, if rescued at all, by the mingling with some purer streams in the lower strata of life. For as the waters are kept pure and sweet by perpetual motion, the blood of men is kept so by continual flowing through the veins of all the nations.

XVIII.

THE FUTURE—NO WHITE, NO BLACK.

There are no insuperable difficulties in the way of this reform. The practice of melaleukation will be first openly adopted in the more thickly populated slave States. It is universal, now, throughout the South and only needs legitimatizing. The irregular alliances of to-day, will become the recognized unions of to-morrow. It has been well said that the slave of yesterday is the soldier of to-day and the citizen of to-morrow. He is to become the social and political equal of the white.

Under the ordinance of nature, confirmed by the solemn act of President Lincoln, in the emancipation proclamation, there are no slaves to-day in law at the South. Slavery is *de jure*, if not *de facto*, dead. This is the first step towards the redemption of the black and his absorption with the white. The second step is in making him a soldier of the United States. If he has fought beside the white, if he has spent his blood for the common country, the most ordinary sense of justice will revolt at the idea of remanding him back to slavery, or of denying him any opportunity or right accorded to his white comrade. If he has the ability in any sphere of industry, or in the development of any of the higher faculties of the mind to outstrip his white brother, he has also the right, and that theory which would deprive him of it is the plea of imbeciles and cowards. The only anomaly in our black army is that it has white officers. This will disappear as time passes by, and the black private and non-commissioned officer shows bravery and skill enough to lead not only men of his own race, but men of the white race. It will be a sad misfortune if this war should end without a battle being fought by a black general in command of a white or mixed body of troops. We want an American Toussaint L'Ouverture, to give the black his proper position on this continent, and the day is coming. People say the Rebellion is at an end, but this is not true. The South will fight to the last, but it is in the eternal fitness of things that they should finally be subdued by the black soldier. When the great armies of the Rebellion are destroyed, and the war resolves itself into guerrilla fighting, the black soldier, who is now in training, will be invaluable to seek out and put down the last remnants of organized force against the

Government. It will then be due to the justice of history, that the Administration put the negro in supreme control of the South. The slave of yesterday not only is the soldier of to-day, but is destined to be the conqueror of to-morrow. The transition from this position to entire social equality will be very easy. The Southern whites will concede the full manhood of those who have met them in honorable conflict and defeated them. The Southern people, because of their intimate personal contact with the colored man, have never learned those prejudices against him which disgrace the North. They will disappear in the North, when the colored people become more numerous here.

It follows, therefore, that after the war is over, the American people will be compelled to apportion the great plantations of the South among their former slaves, who will have won the title by their valor in the field. They will be made not only land-holders, but citizens. They will be eligible to office; to all the rights now possessed wholly by the white race. We shall then, in contested elections, see how eager the white candidate for office will be to prove not only that he is the black man's friend, but that he has black blood in his veins. Even in the last municipal election in New York, Mr. F. I. A. Boole, the candidate of the pro-slavery, Tammany, and Mozart organizations, for the Mayoralty, fearful of a defeat, called together a meeting of the black men, as reported in the Tribune of November 30 and 31, 1863, and besought their influence to elect him, promising to shield them in the exercise of their just rights and privileges, and placing himself on record as a friend of the colored man. During the same week a colored regiment passed through New York unmolested. The riot in that city was an expiring spasm of this prejudice, and had only the effect of increasing the public sentiment of respect and regard for the negroes. By the close of the war the pride of race, founded on an ignorant self-sufficiency, will be forgotten, and give place to a desire to secure his influence, and to become one with him in all the relations of life. The large cities of the South, New Orleans especially, even now swarm with mulattoes, quadroons, octoroons, and all shades of color. The unions producing these mixtures will be continued under the sanctions of public opinion, law, and religion.

Let no one, therefore, take trouble as to the possibility of effecting this great reform. It will work out itself. The course the Government has entered upon leads logically to this result. As the war has progressed, men's minds have been opened more and more to the true cause of our country's difficulties. Human nature is imperfect; it can ordinarily take in only half or quarter truths. It was a great step in the advance when the country willingly accepted the truth that all men should be free. But it might not have been seen by many that further along in the path of Progress we should recognize the great doctrine of human brotherhood, and that human brotherhood comprehended not merely the personal freedom, but the acknowledgment of the political and social rights of the negro, and the provision for his entrance into those family relations which form the dearest and strongest ties that bind humanity together. Once place the races upon a footing of perfect equality, and these results will surely follow.

History presents some curious instances of the effect of law and public opinion in keeping separate or in absorbing a distinct people. The Jews are a peculiar example. Since the time of the destruction of Jerusalem, they have been a marked race upon the earth, and both in Christian and Mahommedan countries have been under the pale of the law and of public opinion. As a consequence they have remained a peculiar people by themselves. Their customs and habits have been different, their very features different, from the masses of people about them. They have come to be hated and despised. America is the first country that has done the Jews justice, and what has been the result? They are equal here socially and politically with other sects, and the Jews in America, as a distinct nation, are dying out. They occupy our public offices, they are lecturers, actors, journalists. The American Jew of the second and third generation cannot be distinguished either by feature or habits from other American citizens. They have already commenced to intermarry, and soon the American Jew will be no more peculiar than the American Methodist or Presbyterian.

The wandering Gipsies or Bohemians, are another instance of the separation and subsequent absorption of a people. During the Middle Ages, and down almost to our time, the Gipsies were a peculiar people—made so by laws and public opinion. George Borrow, in his famous book on the Zincali of Spain, has traced their history for several generations. He shows that they began to disappear in Spain just so soon as the laws in relation to them were abrogated. From that time forth, they mingled with the Spanish people, and are to-day scarcely distinguishable from the other inhabitants of that peninsula. English Gipsies are also fast being absorbed, and in this country they are not known from the rest of the population. In England the Irish are a separate class, degraded as the negro is in the Northern States. But the Irishman who emigrates to America is lost in our population after the first generation. He has here perfect social and political rights, and, as a consequence, is an American citizen, and loses all the peculiarities which render him so disagreeable to the Anglo-Saxon on the other side of the ocean.

Once let the negro become the equal before the law, and the equal in social rights with the white, and he will disappear as a peculiar man, as the Jews and Irish disappear by absorption in America, and as the Gipsies are disappearing under the enlightened public opinion of modern Europe.

Let it be understood, then, that equality before the law, for the negro, secures to him freedom, privilege to secure property and public position, and above all, carries with it the ultimate fusion of the negro and white races. When this shall be accomplished by the inevitable influences of time, all the troubles that loom up now in the future of our country, will have passed away. It is the true solution of our difficulties, and he is blind who does not see it. The President of the United States, fortunately for the country, has made a great advance in the right direction. His first thought in connection with the enfranchisement of the slaves, was to send them from the country. He discovered first, that this was physically impossible, and second that the labor alone which would be lost to America and the world, would amount in value to more than the debts of all the nations of the earth. The negro is rooted on this continent; we cannot remove him; we must not hold him in bondage. The wisest course is to give him his rights, and let him alone; and by the certain influence of our institutions, he will become a component element of the American Man.

XIX.

MISCEGENATION IN THE PRESIDENTIAL CONTEST.

The question of miscegenetic reform should enter into the approaching presidential contest. It is our duty as Americans, as Christians, as humanitarians, to take advantage of the circumstances which Providence has brought about, to introduce a new and improved life on this continent. Slavery no longer exists, but the black man is not yet an equal, before the law, of the white man, nor does custom give him the same social rights. But the times are propitious. If the progressive party of this country have courage, have faith in humanity and in their own doctrines, they can solve the problem which has perplexed our Statesmen since the establishment of the Government. That problem is, What to do with the black race. The slaveholder himself concedes that we require the labor of that race, that we want the thews and sinews of the black man for the cotton he grows, the sugar he produces, the tobacco he reaps, and all the thousand products of the Southern States, which go to fill the coffers of the nation. The mere value of the slave as a laborer, judged by the standard of the ox or horse, was estimated before the war as high as two thousand millions of dollars. His value as a moral and intellectual being is infinitely higher. The value of his blood with the mingled bloods which go to make up the American people, can never be estimated by money. Let the Republican party, then, rise to the height of the great argument; let them recognize the full equality of the negro before the law; let them ordain that, as a matter of simple justice, the man whose toil has enriched the Southern plantations should own them. For three or four generations, the profits of the labor of the slaves of the South have been spent in idleness by a few thousand white families. This great crime against the black man, thanks to the President's proclamation, the confiscation act, and the growing humanity of public opinion at the North, is no longer possible. As a matter of justice, the lands of the South must be divided among the negroes, who are its only loyal population. The work has commenced well at Port Royal, where the negroes are buying from the Government the farms that used to be their masters', and it must be continued throughout the rebel States.

But the negroes have another claim which is indisputable in law or justice—the claim of hereditary descent. Three-fourths of the four millions of the former slaves of the South have the blood of white aristocrats in their veins. They are, as the direct descendents of owners of plantations, entitled to share the property of their fathers, with their white brothers and sisters. It will be a crime for which history will never forgive the American people, if, after the slave oligarchy of the South has raised its hand to strike down the Constitution of the country, and obliterate nearly half of the stars which cluster upon its flag, they should restore it to its old place and power, and turn their backs upon the millions of loyal Africans whose prayers by day and by night have gone up for the success of the banner of Union and Liberty. The platform of the Chicago Convention—how meagre, how mean does it look beside the great result which followed the election of Abraham Lincoln. Let the Republican party go into the next contest with a platform worthy of itself; worthy of the events which have occurred during the last three years; worthy of America, worthy of the great future. Let the motto then of the great progressive party of this country be Freedom, Political and Social Equality ; Universal Brotherhood. Let it send a message to all the nations of the earth, " Come hither with your means, come hither in the strength of your manhood, come hither with the wealth of your varied bloods. Let us establish here a nation founded on the principles of eternal justice, and upon the application of the doctrine of human brotherhood." These are questions, we are aware, that alarm those timid men, that always deprecate any movement toward Reform. They will dread the old prejudices which these subjects will awaken into new activity. But the promulgation of anti-slavery principles excit ed far more intense opposition than these are likely to receive ; because, as time has passed by, and the questions affecting the colored race have been discussed, men have perceived that the hatred of race they indulged in was unworthy of their manhood, and that the negro, if not up to the level of the best specimens of the Caucasian, had all the qualifications which would fit him to be the companion of his white brother.

XX.

AN OMEN.

The statue of Liberty which has just crowned the capitol at Washington, stands as a symbol of the future American of this continent. It was meet and proper that while slavery exercised its baneful sway at the seat of Government, that the great dome of the capitol should have been unfinished, and that the figure of Liberty should not have unveiled its awful form upon the topmost summit. The maker of that statue has "builded better than he knew." In order to insure it against the storms and variable temperature of a Virginia atmosphere, it has been washed with an acid which has caused a slight oxidation, producing a rich and uniform bronze tint, which no rains can discolor and no sun bleach. When the traveler approaches the city of magnificent distances, the seat of what is destined to be the greatest and most beneficent power on earth, the first object that will strike his eye will be the figure of Liberty surmounting the capitol ; not white, symbolizing but one race, nor black typifying another, but a statue representing the composite race, whose sway will extend from the Atlantic to the Pacific ocean, from the Equator to the North Pole—the Miscegens of the Future.

CONCLUSIONS.

In the preceding pages the author has endeavored to make plain the following propositions:

1. That as by the teaching of science, religion, and democracy, the whole human race is of one family, it follows that there should be no distinction in political or social rights on account of color, race, or nativity, in a republic.
2. That the doctrine of human brotherhood should be accepted in its entirety in the United States, and that it implies the right of white and black to intermarry, should they so desire.
3. That the solution of the negro problem will not have been reached in this country, until public opinion sanctions a union of the two races.
4. That, as the negro cannot be driven out of the country, or exterminated, as for a wise purpose he has been placed side by side with the white in the Southern States, there should be no impediment to the absorption of the one race in the other.

5. That whereas, this mingling of races has been going on illegitimately for over a hundred years at the South, without any evil effect, legitimate unions between whites and blacks could not possibly have any worse result than the present system.

6. That the mingling of diverse races is a positive benefit to the progeny, as is proven by the history of all nations, from that of Egypt to the present day.

7. That as the rebellion has been caused not so much by slavery, as the base prejudice resulting from a distinction of color, and that perfect peace cannot be restored to our country until that distinction shall measurably cease, by a general absorption of the black race by the white.

8. That it is the duty of anti-slavery men everywhere to advocate miscegenation, or the mingling of all the races on this continent. It is well to make the negro free, it is better still to make him a soldier, but it is best of all to share with him our hearts and homes.

9. That whereas, the result of the last Presidential election has given the colored race on this continent its freedom, the next Presidential election should secure to every black man and woman the rest of their social and political rights; that the progressive party must rise to the height of the great argument, and not flinch from the conclusions to which they are brought by their own principles.

10. That in the millenial future, the most perfect and highest type of manhood will not be white or black, but brown, or colored, and that whoever helps to unite the various races of men, helps to make the human family the sooner realize its great destiny.

APPENDIX.

TESTIMONY OF WENDELL PHILLIPS.

(*From his Speech at Framingham, Mass., July* 4, 1863.)

Now, I am going to say something that I know will make *The New York Herald* use its small capitals and notes of admiration [Laughter], and yet, no well-informed man this side of China, but believes it in the very core of his heart. That is, "amalgamation"—a word that the Northern apologist for Slavery has always used so glibly, but which you never heard from a Southerner. Amalgamation! Remember this, the youngest of you: that on the 4th day of July, 1863, you heard a man say, that in the light of all history, in virtue of every page he ever read, he was an amalgamationist, to the utmost extent. [Applause.] I have no hope for the future, as this country has no past, and Europe has no past, but in that sublime mingling of races, which is God's own method of civilizing and elevating the world. [Loud applause.] When, therefore, Montgomery Blair, in his speech, libels the amalgamation of races, and slanders the founders of the Constitution, he does what every well-informed man knows that he cannot be ignorant enough really to believe, and what every patriot knows was the basest work that a public man could do in this crisis of our National struggle. God, by the events of his Providence, is crushing out the hatred of race which has crippled this country until to-day. This speech is the effort of the Administration to float into office on a wicked prejudice, the Nation's worst foe; and it aims to keep that prejudice alive in order to make base use of it. The debauched heir who kills his father the sooner to enjoy his estate, is a meek-eyed and lofty saint, compared with an Administration which calls on the negro to save it, and when saved and rich, instead of mercifully killing its benefactor, sends him to penniless and desert exile, while the "dominant and domineering" (God save the mark!) race riots on the spoils it had neither brains, industry, nor courage to win. Know all men, that this meanest of all ingrates, was neither Northener nor Southerner, but born in some nameless region, with neither the honest virtues nor the decent faults of either. 1861 and 1862 saw this war lifted to the august level of a revolution; that speech sinks it to the deadly miasma of the level of politics. If it were possible for man to defeat God, in that speech is the poison. My warning, therefore, is this: Do not despair. An hundred Lincolns, a whole creation of Blairs, could not check the sublime sweep of Niagara, the certain triumph of liberty and justice on this continent. But, at the same time, remember this: the man who, sitting as President, and speaking by the voice of his agent, appeals to that prejudice, to loathsome ignorance, to all the worst enemies of the country, is not to be trusted as a leader. Gen. Butler said to me a fortnight ago—and this is the counterpart of loyalty to treason—Butler said to me, "I am no negro lover, as you are, but before I ask a negro to fight for me, by the living God, he shall have his rights!" [Prolonged applause.] I acknowledge that is a white man, and this speech—the meanest kind of something else. If this is Republicanism, let us ardently pray God for the advent of Democracy. There can be nothing worse.

TESTIMONY OF THEODORE TILTON.

(From his Speech at the Cooper Institute, New York, May 12, 1863, at the Anniversary of the Anti-Slavery Society.)

God, counseling with himself how to crown this people the greatest on the earth, said, "Of what fibre shall I make them?" And he poured into their veins the Saxon blood—painting their eyes with the sky, and gilding their hair with the sun. Then he mingled with it the Celtic, quickened with mercury, and touched with fire. Then he poured into it the sunny wines of the South of Europe. Then, after many other gifts, he added—last but not least—a strange, mysterious current—that bleeds, when wounded, like other men's blood!—that dances in the pulse when joy-smitten, like other men's blood!—yet that carries the blackness of darkness into men's faces, in token that it should also carry the shadow of death into men's souls!

God said, "How shall I prepare a continent to be the home of such a people?" And he ribbed it through the centre with mountain-chains—that the Swiss and the Swede, coming hither, might renew their ancient fellowship with the eternal hills. He salted it on either side with two great seas—that the maritime people of Europe, coming hither, might find still fairer coasts for their ships. He laid his leveling palm upon it, that the Hollander, coming hither, might see the Zuyder Zee, touched by miracle of nature, blooming into an illimitable level of prairie-grass. Last, but not least, he stretched its southern slope into the tropical heats—that the negro also, coming hither, might find a home, where he and the eagle should together look at the sun! * * * The history of the world's civilization is written in one word—which many are afraid to speak—which many more are afraid to hear—and that is Amalgamation. * * * Three stupendous processes of intermingling are going forward in this country, First, we are absorbing the Irish race. Second, we are absorbing the German race. Third, are we absorbing the negro race? No, just the opposite. Look at the facts. It is not black blood that pours itself into white veins. It is white blood that pours itself into black veins. It is not, therefore, a philosophical statement to say, as President Sturtevant says, that the negro race is being absorbed by the white. On the contrary, the negro race is receiving and absorbing part of the white. A large fraction of the white race of the South is melting away into the black. I am not stating any theory on the subject—I am stating only the fact. And this is the plain fact, which no man can gainsay. * * *

Have you not seen with your own eyes—no man can have escaped it—that the black race in this country is losing its typical blackness? Go into any social company of colored people. I was lately amongst them at a wedding—for they, too, marry and are given in marriage. Not one in twenty of the colored persons present had either the pure African hue or feature. What does this argue? That the negro race is passing away, like the Indian? No! the Indian is dying out—the negro is only changing color! Men who, by-and-by, shall ask for the Indians, will be pointed to their graves—"There lie their ashes." Men who, by-and-by, shall ask for the negroes, will be told, "There they go, clad in white men's skins." The negro dying out? Vain thought! The race has not only its own blood to keep it alive, but is taking to itself the blood of the aristocracy of the South. The negro is filling his veins from two fountains of life! A hundred years ago a mulatto was a curiosity—now the mulattoes are half a million. You can yourself predict the future! Mr. Phillips, last evening, held in his hand, on this platform, an early, white, May blossom of the coming harvest. [Referring to the little white slave-girl, whom Mr. Beecher had baptized the Sunday before.]

I am not advocating the union of whites and blacks. This is taking place without advocacy. It neither waits for the permission of an argument in favor of it, nor stays at the barrier of an argument against it. I am often asked, "Would you marry a black woman?" I reply, "I have a wife already, and therefore will not." I am asked, "Do you think that a white man ought ever to marry a black woman? I reply, "When a man and woman want to be married, it is *their* business, not mine, nor anybody's else." Is not that plain sense? But to read what some newspapers say of the "monstrous doctrine of amalgamation," one would think it consisted in stationing a provost-marshal at street corners, to seize first a white man and then a black woman, and to marry them on the spot, against their will, for a testimony to human equality. But I will venture to advance the opinion as holding good in morals, that a slave-woman's master, who makes himself the father of her children, is in honor bound to make himself her husband. So far from denouncing the marriage of blacks and whites, I would be glad if the banns of a hundred thousand such marriages could be published next Sunday, that in many a slave's cabin or master's mansion, the unrepaired wrong might be righted, and the fallen honor raised. But whether in marriage or in shame, the fact grows broader every day, that the whites and the blacks of this country are coalescing; or to use the more horrible word, amalgamating. In Slavery, this amalgamation proceeds rapidly; in Freedom slowly; but it proceeds, nor will it stop. And in the far future, the negro will wash his face into paleness with the blood of white men's veins! * * * I ask, also, that the negro shall be eligible to every political office to which white men are eligible. I do not say that he shall *hold* office, only that he shall be *eligible*. Then, after nomination, if you don't like him, vote him down—as you vote down other decent men. [Laughter.] Are negroes capable of holding office? Capable of governing States? Well, for instance, for the next Presidency, as between Gen. McClellan and Frederick Douglass—who is your choice? [Applause.]

In the British Island of Jamaica, the ablest man in the Government is Sir Edward Jordon—and he is a negro. I hope to see the day when South Carolina shall be governed by some educated negro, lifted to that high position by the generous majority of a free people. [Applause.] But, remember, I do not ask that *competent* black men shall hold office. I ask that *incompetent* black men shall hold office—for only so will they be on a level with the whites. [Laughter.]

I ask that the negro shall receive the respect of the best society. He always does—for that only is the best society that honors the poor! [Applause.] Ask him into your pew at church. Let him ride at your side in the cars. Give him the right hand of fellowship—as indeed, God ordained, for He made the inside of the negro's hand white, for clasping a white man's. [Laughter.] The finest sight I ever saw in Central Park, was an old wagon, drawn by an old horse, with an Irishman and a negro sitting side by side on one seat, taking a fashionable drive. [Laughter.] That team, and its teamsters, I thought, drove further towards the millenium than all the gilded cavalcade that whirled by! [Laughter and applause.]

THE NATIVE INDIAN BLOOD MINGLING WITH THE WHITE.

(From the North British Review.)

The answer to the question, "Is the red race doomed?" which has been given by all writers on the subject, has hitherto been an unhesitating affirmative. Dr. Wilson (in his "Pre-historic Man"), however, presents us with a new, and, we must say, more acceptable view of the case. The Red Men, he says, will indeed disappear, but not wholly by extinction. The diminution of their numbers is being effected, to a considerable extent, by absorption into the race which is supplanting them. This is an entirely new view, and a very important one. Dr. Wilson demonstrates that it is also a true one. * * * Dr. Wilson says :

"At every fresh stage of colonization, or of pioneering into the wild west, the work has necessarily been accomplished by the hardy youths, or the hunters and trappers of the clearing. Rarely indeed, did they carry with them wives or daughters ; but where they found a home amid savage-haunted wilds, they took to themselves wives of the daughters of the soil."

Henry, in his narrative of travel among the Cristineaux, on Lake Winipegon, in 1760, after describing the dress and allurements of the female Cristineaux, adds : "One of their chiefs assured me that the children borne by their women to Europeans, were bolder warriors and better hunters than themselves." * * *

Nowhere is this remarkable process of intermixture and absorption seen on so great a scale as at the Red River settlement, where there is a settled population of mixed blood, amounting to about 7,200 souls, who intermarry freely with the white population, and share with perfect equality in all the rights and privileges of the community. The personal observation of Mr. Morgan and others, show that a partial intermixture of the two races is likewise taking place in the territories of the United States. In the *Varieties of Mankind,* in which the doctrine of the unity of mankind is denied, it is maintained by Dr. Nott, that opposite races, such as the red and the white, cannot amalgamate, for that the offspring of such intermarriages always is feeble and dies out No such hybrid race, he says, can be permanently established; and the red men, in his opinion, were doomed to extinction, without leaving a trace of their existence. The facts brought to lignt by Dr. Wilson, entirely refute these opinions.

Remarkable as are many of the phenomena presented to us in the New World, the most remarkable, as it seems to us, is the extraordinary commingling of diverse races which is being accomplished on its soil. Navigation has now so bridged the ocean, that from every country in Europe, settlers have reached the American shore; and railways have so facilitated locomotion by land, and so quickened the movements of social life, that these diverse people from Europe are shaken together and amalgamated in the New World, till the original distinctions disappear, and a new national type is formed. Moreover, as we have seen, these white Americans are blending to some extent with the native red stock of the continent. Within a century from the present time, we may expect to see the separate existence of the red man and his hunting-grounds swept away, and an ethnographically composite, yet socially homogeneous population, existing all over North America. The intermingled white blood of Europe will here and there be tinged with the native red blood of America. Nor does the strange commixture of population stop here. *Not only Europe and America, but Africa, and in a lesser degree Asia, will be represented in the new race which is growing up in the New World.* The Chinese settlers in California are the vanguard of a more numerous emigration, which will, ere long, take place from the crowded fields of China to the American shores of the Pacific.

INTERMINGLING OF COLORS AND SEXES AT OBERLIN UNIVERSITY.

(Correspondence of the "Independent.")

The peculiarities of Oberlin are its intermingling of the sexes, its free admission of colored students, its peculiarly religious life, and its theological tenets. * * *

I attended prayers in the college chapel Saturday evening. It was full. On one side of the house sat young ladies; on the other young gentlemen. Out of an audience of six or seven hundred, perhaps twenty or thirty were colored men and women. They sat intermingled with their comrades. They are treated as friends. The principles of the college and the spirit of the people alike forbid all insult or rudeness to them. In a period of thirty years, the effect of this association of sexes and colors has not proved disastrous. The reverse is true. The whites find their prejudice melting away under the influence of kindly, social intermingling; the blacks receive a culture which no mere colored school could afford them; while the intermingling of young men and women acts as a healthful inspiration and restraint upon both.

THE NEGRO ARTIST OF THE STATUE OF LIBERTY ON THE CAPITOL.

(*Washington correspondence of N. Y. Tribune, December* 2, 1863.)

When the bronze castings were being completed at the foundry of Mr. Mills, near Bladensburg, his foreman, who had superintended the work from the beginning, and who was receiving eight dollars per day, struck, and demanded ten dollars, assuring Mr. M. that the advance must be granted to him, as nobody in America, except himself could complete the work. Mr. M. felt that the demand was exorbitant, and appealed in his dilemma to the slaves who were assisting in the moulding. "I can do that well," said one of them, an intelligent and ingenious servant, who had been intimately engaged in the various processes. The striker was dismissed, and the negro, assisted occasionally by the finer skill of his master, took the striker's place as superintendent, and the work went on. The black master-builder lifted the ponderous, uncouth masses, and bolted them together, joint to joint, piece by piece, till they blended into the majestic "Freedom," who to-day lifts her head in the blue clouds above Washington, invoking a benediction upon the imperiled Republic!

Was there a prophecy in that moment when the slave became the artist, and with rare poetic justice, reconstructed the beautiful symbol of freedom for America?

HARRIET BEECHER STOWE'S PEN-PORTRAIT OF A MISCEGENETIC WOMAN AND MAN.

[The following extracts from "Dred" give a very imperfect idea of the characters of the man and woman of mixed bloods, whom she places among the central figures of her book, and who are, of course, more fully portrayed in the narrative than in these brief descriptions. They are known as Harry, the quadroon overseer of Colonel Gordon's estate, and Lisette, his wife.]

LISETTE.

She was a delicate, airy little creature, formed by a mixture of the African and French blood, producing one of those fanciful, exotic combinations, that gives the same impression of brilliancy and richness that one receives from tropical insects and flowers. From both parent races she was endowed with a sensuous being, exquisitely quick and fine, a nature of everlasting childhood, with all its freshness of present life, all its thoughtless, unreasoning fearlessness of the future. She stands there at her ironing table, just outside her cottage door, singing gaily at her work. Her round, plump, childish form is shown to advantage by the trim blue basque, laced in front over a chemisette of white linen. Her head is wreathed with a gay turban, from which escapes, now and then, a wandering curl of her silky black hair. Her eyes, as she raises them, have the hazy, dreamy languor, which is so characteristic of the mixed races.

HARRY.

The young man was a well-dressed, gentlemanly person of about thirty-five, with dark complexion and hair, and deep, full, blue eyes. There was something marked and peculiar in the square, high forehead, and the finely formed features, which indicated talent and ability, and the blue eyes had a depth and strength of color that might cause them at first to appear black. * * * * At Colonel Gordon's death, he had bequeathed, as we have already shown, the whole family estate to his daughter, under the care of a servant, of whose uncommon intelligence and thorough devotion of heart he had the most ample proof. When it is reflected that the overseers are generally taken from a class of whites who are often lower in ignorance and barbarism than even the slaves, and that their wastefulness and rapacity are a byword among planters, it is no wonder that Colonel Gordon thought that, in leaving his plantation under the care of one so energetic, competent, and faithful as Harry, he made the best possible provision for his daughter.

Henry was the son of his master, and inherited much of the temper and constitution of his father, tempered by the soft and genial temperament of the beautiful Eboe mulattress, who was his mother. From this circumstance, Harry had received advantages of education very superior to what commonly fall to the lot of his class. He had also accompanied his master as valet, during the tour of Europe, and thus his opportunities of general observation had been still further enlarged, and that tact, by which those of the mixed blood seem so peculiarly fitted to appreciate all the finer aspects of conventional life, had been called out and exercised, so that it would be difficult in any circle to meet with a more agreeable or gentlemanly person. * * * Possessed of uncommon judgment, firmness, and knowledge of human nature, Harry had found means to acquire great ascendancy over the hands of the plantation, and either through fear or through friendship, there was a universal subordination to him.

www.ingramcontent.com/pod-product-compliance
Lightning Source LLC
Chambersburg PA
CBHW051504270326
41933CB00021BA/3461
9781639237555